How He Loved Them

Also by Kevin Prufer:

Churches
In a Beautiful Country
National Anthem
Fallen from a Chariot
The Finger Bone
Strange Wood

How He Loved Them

Kevin Prufer

Four Way Books

Tribeca

Library of Congress Cataloging-in-Publication Data

Names: Prufer, Kevin, author.
Title: How he loved them / Kevin Prufer.
Description: New York, NY : Four Way Books, [2018]
Identifiers: LCCN 2017029366 | ISBN 9781945588099 (softcover : acid free paper)
Classification: LCC PS3566.R814 A6 2018 | DDC 811/.54--dc23
LC record available at https://lccn.loc.gov/2017029366

This book is manufactured in the United States of America and printed on acid-free paper.

Four Way Books is a not-for-profit literary press. We are grateful for the assistance we receive from individual donors, public arts agencies, and private foundations.

PROUD MEMBER

We are a proud member of the Community of Literary Magazines and Presses.

Distributed by University Press of New England
One Court Street, Lebanon, NH 03766

Contents

•

• •

• • •

How He Loved Them

How much the colonel loved his granddaughters
you will never know.
                    Their laughter filled his black Mercedes
the way a flock of starlings might fill a single tree
with song.
            What he'd had to do that day, he'd done
with a troubled heart,
                    but now their laughter overwhelmed him
with such inarticulable love
                    he could hardly
contain it
            and neither could the empathetic little bomb
in the engine,
            which chose that moment
to burst through the hood with self-obliterating joy.

+

And the Mercedes burned in front of the courthouse.

And the black smoke billowed and rose like a heart full of love.

And the colonel rose, too,
                    like burning newspaper

caught in the wind,

                a scrap of soot, then nothing, then unknowable—

+

You will never know

              what dying is like.

The colonel's granddaughters are still laughing in the backseat,

or they are uncomfortable in the new bodies
the bomb made for them.

Oh, darling, darling, one of them recalled,
you are burning up

                 with fever—her mother's cool hand on her forehead,
then the sense of slipping under,

                      into black sleep. *She's asleep now,*
the voice said, turning out the light,

                    closing the door.

+

And in every hand, smartphones made footage
of their bodies,

        the heaps and twists of metal.

The smoke uploaded the wreckage

                to the screenlike sky
where it goes on burning forever—

You will never know if dying is like that,
the same scenes repeated across a larger mind

                  than yours—

+

Is it like a small girl with a high fever asleep in a dark room
recollected for a moment

           as the brain closes down?
She's asleep, the voices say, *she's resting.*

(*My fleeting one, my obliterated device, my bit of pixilated
soot.*) Hit *Pause*

          and the smoke stops: a black pillar
that weighs the wreckage down.

              Then *Play*—

how much he loved them,

                    unknowable—

+

What the colonel had done that day

                        had troubled his heart,
but the sound of his granddaughters' laughter
lifted him high into the air

                  like a scrap of burning paper
blown from the street into the trees.

Ars Poetica

I slept in a far-away tent, I slept in a hollow log, then I slept in a crate
abandoned in the snow,

I built my shelter from garbage and branches, I slept in the truckyard's
pile of tires, I slogged through the marsh, upsetting the herons—

before I knew you, I owned a gun, before I knew you, I kept a sparrow in
a shoebox, I fed it ham and held it to my head to hear it sing,

I called it a radio, it kept the blues away, I called it love and wrote down
all the words,

I loved sad songs and I carried a gun before I knew you, and, Lord, when
they shipped me here,

I roamed hotel hallways dazzle-eyed and strange, I pushed a cart full of
towels, gun-in-my-pocket,

I made the beds, I missed my friends, I missed my crate, my pile of tires,
I had such friends

before they shipped me here, Lord, Tampa, Cincinnati, Sparks, ear to my
radio,

I am old and wounded in the thigh, I listen to the ice machine's clinking thoughts, I push my cart

while the planes take off, low and thundering toward the distant edge, Lord,

there's no gun in my hand, it's a box of notes, a simple record of my time.

After You Have Gone

The little red jewel in the bottom of your wineglass
is so lovely I cannot rinse it out,

so I go into the cool and grassy air to smoke.
Which one is your warmly lit house

past which soldiers no longer march?
When you reached across the table to touch my hand

is not attainable. I cannot re-capture it.

And no gunners lean on their artillery at the city's edge,
looking this direction,

having shot the sky full of bright holes.

The light bleeds from them.
Long ago, they captured our city

and now they are our neighbors,
going about their business as if they were one of us.

Soon, like you, they will be asleep,
having washed the dishes and turned out the kitchen lights.

When I inhale, smoke occupies me.
When I exhale—

By morning the wine in the bottom of your glass
will have clotted.

I'm sorry I called it a jewel.
It's not the soldiers who have shot me full of holes.

It's not light that pours out.
Love did this.

I was filled with wine.
Now I'm drained of it.

Black Woods

Do you know where our child has gone?
I'm sorry. Do you know what has become
of him? *I'm sorry.* [.] Is he hiding
in a closet? *No.* Is he crouched among
the shoes? *No.* [.] Should we look
in the closets? *He's not in the closets.* [.]
Should we check the empty boxes? *He's not
in the empty boxes.* It's very cold out. [.]
Probably he's hiding behind the couch.
Come out, come out! I will count to ten.
One, two, three—*He's not behind the couch.*
[.] It's very cold out. [.] Probably
he's playing a trick. *It isn't a trick.* He's probably
hiding above the ceiling tiles. Hello up there!
He's not in the ceiling. [.] It's very cold out.
[.] Did he go out? *No.* Was he wearing
a jacket? *No.* Was he wearing boots
and a hat? [.] It's just black woods
out there. [.] Did you give him your jacket?
[.] Did you offer him your jacket? [.]
Maybe he's in disguise. *Disguise?* In your hat
and jacket. *Disguised?* [.] Disguised
as you. [.] Did he climb through your window?
Listen to yourself. Did he step inside you?

Listen to yourself. Is he trapped inside you?
Let go of me. Is it black woods in there?

Chandler Brossard

When I was twenty
            and desperate and broke,
I worked part-time in a used bookstore
in Middletown, CT.
            I hated my job, hated the cramped store,
hated the paperbacks
            that came there as if to die

+

and more than anything,
I wanted to write something lasting,

a novel I scrawled in notebooks
            called "Black Wing"
about a dark-haired girl,
prized during the day for her beauty and intellect,
who by night
            killed off poseurs, the ill-read, the clumsy-of-mind,
the bombastic, thick-fingered, and mean.

+

Somehow, through incompetence or charity,
the young woman who owned the store

                        never quite fired me

+

though one morning, I found an old man
at my place at the cash register.

He wore a tight leather jacket, a turtleneck,
a gray moustache,
                    and when he saw me,
he took off his glasses
and set his book down on the dust-speckled counter.

This is Chandler Brossard,
the owner told me.
                You'll work with him now.
He looked pale and sick.

+

It was meant to transcend mystery,
                        it was meant to

live in contradictions, to be existential and enigmatic—
the dark-haired girl

            destroying what was not beautiful
and the one-legged detective who pursued her,
but could never apprehend her—

+

            Chandler Brossard,
thin-faced and coughing,
            Chandler Brossard tilted back in his chair,
reading a book in the sun-lit dust motes, *What are you writing?*
he asked me one day,
         and I closed my notebook.
Nothing, I said,
       looking at what age had done to his hands—

+

          He was, the owner told me,
a famous writer once,
        but now he was dying. Chandler Brossard's
Who Walk in Darkness grew yellow
on the shelf.

And he smelled like an old man,
Vicks VapoRub and snuff

        and mint—

+

How the knife comes down, I thought,
typing away that night

        while one of my roommates
burned his fingers on a joint

        and the other
practiced his guitar—

        How the knife comes down
in the flesh of the critic,

        in the sycophant, the vulgar,
and the room grew colder
because no one paid our bills—

+

        and I wanted Chandler Brossard
to say something wise

        but he was just an old man.

And when I finally told him about "Black Wing"
the plot seemed suddenly

                  contrived,
ugly truth pursuing beauty, beauty
making our foibles

                clear, the dark-haired girl
who posed the horrible bodies

                      for the one-legged detective to
discover—

+

        By then, I'd read one of Brossard's novels
and found it full of squalor,

                familiar—

And he'd grown sicker, pale and unsteady,
though he still walked from the hospital each morning
and sat behind the counter selling paperbacks.

My boss didn't know I'd been kicked out of my apartment,
that when I couldn't find a friend to put me up,
I unrolled a sleeping bag in the bookstore

+

and what I remember most about those sad days
is lying on the floor
                        among stacks of dying books,
the sense of them rising above me in darkness.
So many minds at work,
                        so much trapped thought,

+

while at his apartment,
Chandler Brossard had a few months to live

+

and I slipped into sleep, dreamed of dark-haired
angels,
            angels of squalor, angels of anger and forgetfulness
and sudden mercy
                        in the black air above my head,
angels descending
                        to smother me with beauty
and ambition and paper wings—

+

                              and even if the detective
caught her, what then?
                    Would he know something more
about immortal beauty?

+

He would still be nothing,
a dying, childless old man
who had preserved a bit of himself in a book—

+

Immortality figured as the workings of a mind
                              caught in the sunlit trap
of prose—
          how I wanted that to be true—

+

that sense of eternal light streaming
through store windows,

       its fingers playing over my face,

warm and gentle, the scent of books and dust—
how lovely to lie there without meaning or ambition,
how deathless—

    and Chandler Brossard
standing over me,

      kicking me gently awake
with his boot.

Deep Sea Pod

He'd lost radio contact
                    and down his sea pod sank
into static and spit, the dashboard needle
spinning on its glowing dial.
                    The headset said, *Hush, hush,*
and when he flipped the floodlights on
such creatures splayed their suckers on the glass,
pressed their mouths against the glass—
needle teeth, flagellitic
                    and translucent.

And when he turned the floodlights off,
that sense of falling,
                    the crack of rivets
tightening in their joints.

+

Far above,
          the chief engineer turned the radio's dial.
Hello, she said,
          heart chipping away at her chest. *Hello?*
A crowd had gathered around the radio now.
Come on, she said—

+

while the ocean squeezed him in its fist

                              and he turned the dial
so his headset clicked.

                    The pod was listing now, was rolling,
so he knew he'd come unhitched,
his lifeline torn and dangling in the ocean's upper currents,

+

while high above,

                    the crew had gathered on the deck.
They hauled the cable in

                    and saw how it had torn,
its metal twisted where the pull had been
too much,

          the fiberoptic wires that ran its length
split and useless.

                    Their radio hissed. The pod,
the engineer knew, could not suspend

                              five hundred fathoms down,
but tumbled

          freely into rift and ground—

+

He was a cardboard box a child had buried in a field,
a box of little bones;

he was a human heart, hammering
in someone else's chest.

A chick pecked at its egg's thin wall,
but couldn't break through.

And how the mind would love
to rise from the skull.

+

The engineer wouldn't answer the door
or pick up the phone.

She poured herself a drink,
another.

In her head, the pod tumbled through fields
of murk,

paramecium and scrim, diatomic silt. And when
she slept,

her heart grew thick and banged
against the casing—

+

Hello? Hello?
          The rivets creaked again. *It's only me calling,*
it's only me. Yes, yes.
                    I can hardly hear you. Speak up!
And when the braincase finally caved,

                                        its rivets

split their metal plates
then dug into the silt.

+

Then, all night long,
               her heart attacked her chest
until it cracked her ribs and skin and rose into the air,
wet and empty.
               Her arteries
tethered it to her, so it hovered there, strung.

A passing thought: a little man
might feel quite safe
                    in the hollow of it.

Love Poem: Just Then

Just as the young man pulled the Glock from his jacket
and aimed it at the cashier's head,

at the very moment he balanced the gun just so,
but before he could say a word,

while outside the sun slipped from a cloud
and brightened the parking lot's windshields,

just as the old man at the register realized
exactly what was going to happen next,

to him, to his head, the way it would feel,
concussive, just then, far away,

you lay in bed having just made love,
the sound of him washing himself

in the bathroom, his gentle cough,
just as you contemplated opening the blinds

to let a little sun in, just then, the sun
holding its breath, stillness, stillness, the cool

noise of water, just then I was writing
about how I missed you and wanted you back,

how could I not have you back?
how could I not take you back?

just then, that young man opened the door
and walked right into my sunlit poem

and drew his gun on the old clerk
who held up his hands, said, *Stop,*

I'll give you whatever you want, I'll give you
everything you want—

and even the bullet, snug in its chamber,
couldn't believe what would happen next,

what it would become: a sunburst, an idea,
a sort of pathway.

Could Someone Please Check on My Mother?

When the young man thought about the history of poetry,
it seemed to him he had walked into a crowded room
in which everyone was speaking at once. There was,
he decided, no order to it. And this troubled him
because he had grown used to the idea that one poetry
emerged from another,

                that the history of literature
might be read backwards

                    as each dominant worldview
shrank into a radical poetic sensibility

                        then disappeared
into the great maw

            of the previous generation's
sensibility,

        forever and ever amen.

+

When the social worker found her,
the old woman had been locked in her apartment for four days.
Where is my daughter? she asked, *Where is my daughter?*

—but her pregnant daughter had run off to Atlantic City
with a man she barely knew

and was just then recovering from a car accident
in a strange hospital room, alone.

When the night nurse knocked on the door,
the daughter asked if someone

could please check on her mother.

+

The young man wanted poetry to be like
a congregation in a church
awaiting the moment
                    when the pastor says,
Please rise,
          says, *Now we will sing,*
and the church is full of song.

The pastor, in this metaphor, stands for the poet.
The congregation is language. The church is history.
The hymnals they are holding are what?

Where did the hymnals come from? He didn't know
what to make of the hymnals!

Thus are poems enculturated,
thus are they written by enormous invisible forces
across the great page of humanity,

the congregation singing from identical hymnals
gloriously unto god

until the metaphor fails completely.

+

It was supposed to be a one-night trip,
she told the officer who stood beside her hospital bed,
how could she predict a car wreck?

And her drunk boyfriend couldn't exactly stick around—

Her mother was senile and mean,
so now and then she locked her in her apartment
and took a personal day—

She'd left plenty of food,
the old woman was probably
just fine,

but if you could send someone to check,
it's been four days,
                    I'd be very grateful—

+

Because all the hymnals were the same,
and tucked away,

because the pastor was alone in the sacristy
talking to himself
                    to keep from crying—

And on the ceiling
someone had painted the night sky

and even in darkness, the church windows seemed to glow.

Earlier that day, he'd buried his mother,
and then he'd come to the hushed church
as usual—

+

Poetry was maybe the sound of the pastor,
who thought he was alone,

                    crying to himself in his church,
recollected years later

                by the young man who'd overheard him
and sat now, lost in thought before his newspaper.

+

And when the social worker
unlocked the apartment door,
she found the old woman

                asleep in a square of light
on the floor beneath the window.

She'd been reading her Bible,
the crumpled pages of which lay beside her as if
she'd torn them out one by one.

Where, she asked,
is my daughter? Where
is my daughter,

             even after she'd
been moved to a temporary shelter,

bathed, fed

       at the state's expense—

+

which is how the young man came to read about her case
in the newspaper—

           so hard to be old and abandoned
and voiceless,

        a pregnant daughter
recovering in Atlantic City,

            such silence,

all the measureless churches—
he tried to conceive of them, like silhouettes
through which real people have moved

                and keep moving,

a poem in the mind.

The Old Poets

The vampires were climbing the hill.

+

The little boy, awake late in his tree house,
watched them attain the summit,
first one, then another, then several vampires
silhouetted in the moonlight.

+

I am reminded of my father,
how he walked a similar path through his dusk
while the autumn leaves fell around him;
I was, I fear, one of many small disappointments for that modest man,
one of the vampires said.

+

Soon, the area below his tree house
was crowded with white-faced vampires
looking pensively toward the distance.

+

A lovely moon half-concealed
by the chimneys of that power plant
is also a small disappointment,
another vampire said.

+

Regret, a third whispered, is the rain in the trees,
is those lightning bugs obscured by that bush,
is an empty car left by the side of a busy freeway
far from this hill.

+

The vampires smelled like the warm meals
of their vanished childhoods.

+

They sniffed the air. The boy, they sensed,
would grow old one day, would sit on his porch
looking over the back yard, toward the blinking lights
of his mortgaged youth.

+

Some of the vampires wrote this on little pads
they otherwise kept in their breast pockets.

+

In the tree house, the boy had tacked a cat's pelt
to the wall. He'd spent all day gutting and cleaning,
smoothing it with stones. Now he smiled
as he stroked it with his fingertips.

+

Of all his many pelts, this was the finest.

House Sitter

After her fifth drink she felt lightheaded
and hadn't the strength to climb out of the hot tub.

So good
              just to rest there,
leaning back in the water.

And then she couldn't open her eyes—they'd grown
hot, her whole body emptied,
                               soothed and glowing,

and lovely
              to listen to the water churn,
the gentle pulse that emptied her of words,

until a feeling, like static, overwhelmed her
and she slipped
                   underwater.

+

The little yellow jewel in the bottom of her glass said,
That was easy.

The ounce of liquor that sweetened the bottle:
Too, too easy—

And the drowned woman in the hot tub shifted in its currents,
staring at the starry sky—

+

For a few nights, raindrops disturbed the water's surface.
So much rain that season,
                                        then dying leaves
thickening the lens she looked through.

A wind had toppled the wine glass
                                                that lived now in its surprising
shards. *Nothing to it,*
                        the bottle replied
from the hot tub's edge.

+

The water turned her over in its mind
like an idea,
                easily grasped at first,

but later filled with complexities it hadn't considered:
What had powered her laughter

                               and where did it go?
Her cell phone long ago stopped ringing.
Why?

        At what point
was she no longer herself?

                        At what point
did she become merely

                the hot tub's contents?

+

She is a useful metaphor for me
when I think of people I have loved
who now are gone.

                Memories of the dead
fill us as a body fills a tub. In the process, they displace
other thoughts and memories.

For instance:
listening to rain tap on the windows
or surprised by the first scent of fall,

I want my father back.
And so experience my father's absence
as a displacement
                    of volume.

+

Nothing to it, the bottle said,
half-filled with murky rainwater—

+

So the dead woman grows blue
and foreign as the leaves
                    cover her up. She changes
shape within the mind that holds her, she leaks.

I wish I could believe we are held within the minds of others
and never vanish.

+

And what about the owner of the house?
He had enjoyed a lovely time away
and now, after a month,

                          returned to find
the hot tub churning and uncovered.

And when he swept the leaf rot from the water's surface
and looked down into the brown

                                depth,

he felt only horror.

                    A leg, atilt. Fingers split.
A swirl of half-concealing hair:
the water holding her in its thoughts.

+

I'm still talking about my father.
I think I've exposed myself too much here.

••

Love Poem

It's cold by the highway and I love your steel mills,
how the smokestacks choke the sky with love,
how they wrap their arms around me, oh, America, I love
your lines of trucks—they beat the pavement like hearts full of love
where we hold hands like lovers and stroll among airplanes,
where we linger by hangars, our bodies smoked with love,
then I love you as the bomb loves its timer, as the helmet loves the head,
so when it finally snows, you're the obliterating shrapnel that I love,
you're the falling burning leaves, the great flag on fire, shower of sparks,
you're the green mist the planes emit over the sleeping city
one night not long from now just before dawn—a thin green ice
encasing the buildings, and, America, I'm half-drunk and improvising,
I've walked your frozen highways in snowfall, in ashfall,
I've got you inside me, I'm breathing your tinted air.

Three Metaphors for the Mind at War

I.

As you went on about the war,
a wasp crawled along the lip
of your bottle of wine. It tested the rim for sugar,
rose heavily into sunlight, then landed on the same spot again.
When it finally slipped inside the bottle,
I replaced the cork, then watched it hover behind glass.
You were too wrapped up in your thoughts to notice
how it touched the liquid's surface, rose again,
up and down, muddled and drunk,
looking out of the bottle into thick, green air.
This, I thought, is what passes for thinking these days.

2.

Weeks had passed, and now
so many leaves floated on the hot tub's surface
that it could no longer reflect the clouds and stars
but looked into itself instead
like that old man I once told you about
who left his smoking car overturned in a ditch
and walked the last mile to Jonesboro to sit at the bar
and tell me about his fucked-up childhood.

It was fall then, too, and I think he'd been drunk
all day. He's probably dead by now. A sharp scent
of decay mixed with burning leaves—.
Anyway, the owner had been called to war
and no one had cleaned the hot tub for weeks.
Beneath that carpet of leaves,
the water turned green and poisonous.

3.

Now, you have been dead for years
and I keep your watch in a box on my desk. The battery
goes on and on. Since then,
we have been bombing and bombing other countries.
Some of our bombs have cameras on them, so we can share
their last obliterating thoughts. Were you alive,
you and I would drink our anger until we could barely stand.
The thing about a watch in a box is that,
like you, it tells the same story over and over again
to no one. The battery sends this little pulse
to its brain. The bombs, also, keep falling.
That is their mission and they don't need to think about it
very much.

Immigration

When the wheels came down over Miami
the stowaway in the landing gear,
half-frozen and unconscious,
slipped from the wheel well into blue air.
How amazed he must have been
to wake to that falling sensation
and the rapidly approaching sodium lamps
of the airport parking lot.

The couple that owned the car his body crushed
was astonished at the twist of fate
that brought his life so forcefully into theirs.
Their young son would always remember it,
how just then the cold shadow of another airplane
passed over him, how the bits of jewel-like glass
lay strewn across the asphalt
like the dead man's thoughts.

In the Wheat Field

"It's your rabbit," the officer told the soldier
who pointed his rifle at the fleeing enemy
child. The child was quick in the wheat,
so it took three shots before he tumbled
into the afterlife. Many years later
I put down my book about the war
and walk under the oaks' black branches
to where the snow has capped all the cars
in the elementary school parking lot.
The rooftops glitter meanly.
I have never killed anything and
look at me. I am like the boss of hell.
In the silent movie, the moon
took a rocket to the face and never
stopped smiling. Tonight its ashes
scatter over the rooftops. No, that's snow.
Of all the people he murdered,
that soldier could not forget how
the child swayed a moment in the wheat
before disappearing under the sea of it.
I once found a bullet casing right here
on this sidewalk and, not far from it,
a stain. How could I not imagine
the rest of that story? The cars

grow cool and dire in the parking lot,
and the sodium lights hum like enormous
insects. The soldier wrote a whole book about
what he had done, but it didn't help.
Come on and snow all over me,
come on and shower me with ash.
The sky is bone. The moon is a hole
in somebody's skull.

Overheard at a Restaurant

Just a glass of water for me, thank you.
One ice cube. Thanks. Just one.
But please order what you want. Don't be shy.
And don't worry about me. I'm keeping trim for our troops.
That ribeye looks promising, though, doesn't it? The charcuterie platter?
The bay shrimp in a nest of deconstructed kale, drizzled with truffle oil?
It's nice to have you home for a few days.
Did you read about how they beheaded another captured soldier?
Cut his head right off, clean as you like. I know, it's
terrible. Awful, really. It ought to be a crime,
but the water flushes me out, gives me a kind of inner peace.
All this war must have been hard on you,
the bodies and IEDs and the threatening
music. It certainly has been hard on our nation, and we weren't even
there. Broccolini, yes. You should have that.
And the foie gras on toast with foraged mushrooms and lemon foam,
you should try those, too. And look at those cauliflower florets,
like petite puffs of smoke! The raviolini afloat in broth
like misfired paratroopers! Did you read how they sliced
his head right off? You should eat! They'll send you back
and you'll be nothing but bones.

Civilization

One young thug smashed the Hyundai's headlight with a baseball bat
while the other called his girlfriend on the phone.

(Blinding the Cyclops, Odysseus made a point about civilization.
The Cyclops threw stones in the direction of his ship.)

The moon said *Hi*.

The car burned quietly in the alley until the heat reached the gas tank,
while the other cars did nothing but watch.

(Civilization requires, first of all, the coming together of many
in cooperative assembly.)

The moon said *Here I am, behind this cloud*.

The reporter watched from a distance
while her cameraman uploaded footage of burning cars.

(The further his ship drew from that uncivilized place,
the more insignificant the weeping Cyclops seemed to Odysseus,
who busied himself with his maps.)

The moon rolled through black mists
sprinkling us with sleeping powder.

After a while, one part of the city was thick with smoke
while the other part watched the first part on TV.

(Was it blood or tears that dampened the Cyclops' cheek?
All he knew was he was completely alone,
and he'd never see the blue fog float up from the sea again.)

The moon blinked angrily through smoke.

The television peered into the quiet room
where no one changed the channel.

(The Cyclops collapsed on the beach
and, with his enormous hand, covered up his empty socket.)

After a while, the moon, too, went black in its socket.

I've seen enough, one of us said,
so you turned off the TV
and then the lights.

The New Poets

We were the infirm, cackle-voiced lispers, half-gone in the brain,
gray-headed limpers.

                 Bat-minded and pale, we slept
most days in our chambers, dosed on the cupfuls of pills
they left on our trays.

                 Nights, we wandered

+

vast hallways

            past parked ventilators, past restrooms
and gurneys, the stairwells, the dead elevators.

                         When the bombs
fell, we were very afraid.

+

            From my window, I saw
the overpass crumble.

            The cars slid off like pills from a tray.
And up rose the smoke from a block of sick houses,
up coughed black smoke

               from the maternity ward,
up with the smoke from the row of sad windows,

and the low clouds reflected the orange of their flames.

+

Now we're forgotten,
                    who never mattered much:
Estelle with her puzzles and long lists of words
                                and Grace with her belly
she wraps in a truss. Or nimble old Carl
who climbs out a window
                    to perch on the rooftop
and sing like a bird.

Another Love Poem

A spot of blood
on the cutting board
beside the sliced apple,

and you in the bathroom
wrapping your finger
in gauze—I'm sorry

about what I said.
The kitchen window
downloads sunlight

right into my brain.
The laptop says
they are cutting off

people's heads
again. The bloodspot
gazes at the blue ceiling

where no one
parts the clouds or explains
what the fuck

we are doing
over there. I can't stand it
anymore, the sliced

apple is also stained
right on its big white
smile. I'm sorry,

I should shut up
about the war
and just be grateful

for the Sunday morning
sun and all. Please come back,
have breakfast with me.

Commerce

Something hit the office window hard
so now there's a smear
that won't be washed away
until it rains.

Red & vaguely
heart-shaped, it appears
to hover over
the city like someone's idea

of love. Far below
the morning grows moneyed & quiet,
the last of us
having emerged from our tunnels

& ridden
the long elevators up our buildings'
throats. Even the birds
are at peace on our distant

trees & power lines.
When the keyboards' noise
resumes, I play through
the scene again—

the silent towers, a crack
against the bright glass,
& a burst of black
feathers.

True Crime

One rich motherfucker bashed another rich motherfucker's face in with
a gold-plated putter

so the golf club's snack bar was all atwitter

because who knew? Right here at Briar Cliffe Acres?

Good God, said the river.

Good God, said the wind in the pennant, the yacht at the dock. One
forensic examiner

filled the sand trap with sodium light while another

dusted a nine iron with fingerprint powder.

The half-plastered ladies in tennis whites at the taped-off perimeter

whispered among themselves, *How sad*. And, *Here is a dollar*,

the birds called to each other, pulling grubs from holes in the oak trees.
Here is a dollar,

a dollar, a dollar.

And one squirrel, burying his nut in the weedy grass by the water hazard, muttered,

Got one, then went off in search of another.

And when for a moment the sun disappeared behind a cloud and rain watered

the fairway, the Bermuda grass grew greener, thicker and louder

with providence. With God's holy love. Oh rich motherfuckers,

we live in a world of wealth and thunder.

Just ask the rat and his hole full of plunder. Ask the beaver

and his barge of sticks. One of you may be conked beside the golf cart's tire, but the other

has two tickets to Zürich, one for himself and one for the dead man's daughter.

Such bounty. The sun gilds us until we glitter.

Marvelous Ships

If you'll just swipe your card, if you'll enter your destination, if you'll look into the camera, if you'll put your eye to the glass, steady, steady, you will see a light—

their terrifying ships having sailed, taking many of us away—what could we do but go about our business on the shore?

(but in those awful days, they closed all the airports and such lines at the gas pumps, do you remember the lines?)

has this suitcase always been in your possession? did you pack it yourself? will you open it?

though at night we built bonfires on the beach from the brush we gathered, and in their glow we told stories of those who had been taken—

(strange to think of the empty airports, one gate after the next, light sliding through enormous windows, the conveyer belts stopped,)

why are you sweating, sir, it's a simple question, a *yes* or *no* will do,

their enormous masts pointing skywards, their cannons, we had no choice—each time they came, we brought them living bodies, for which we received amulets and knives—

(those empty airports in the outskirts—you don't remember, once they were glorious with people)

we're going to ask you to step away from the counter, sir, we're going to ask you to hold your hands behind your head, sir,

and in many ways we prospered under their dominion—

(empty as sighs, empty as pockets)

we're going to ask you to come with us, sir, we're going to ask you not to resist or create a scene,

and in this way, you, too, have benefitted from the arrangement, which has taken on the quality of tradition—

(I saw an airplane grow wind-bitten, its wing collapsing on the runway, when the ice came its hull glittered in sunlight)

if the next in line will swipe his card, if the next in line—

if you'll step aboard this marvelous ship.

•••

Monkey Lab

Remove the animal skullplate. Inside,

                                  his brain turns in its sugar.

Touch it.

          A tension at the wrists' restraints.

Odd topography,
the brain adrift beneath its holed bone sky,

                             creeks and mountains

ruffling the surface. Poke it

                 with a pin. His eyes blink

and widen. His mouth says *oh!*—

                    the way beauty sounds

poured through the senses—a gasp and *oh!* Such colors

among the wrinkled mountains,

                    sweetness for the eye

when the pin goes in.

+

What kind of a God are you?

                  He was your bag

of blood and bone,

         you carried him from his cage, he was your

thick-tongued, drugged, perceiving

                machine.

+

In a magazine in the doctor's waiting room,
a photograph of a monkey locked in a plastic chair,
his skull open like a box, eyes

                astonished—I couldn't put it down.
The thin-gloved fingers
that shaved the head, then held the skinflap back—

My father, who would not live long,
dozing in his wheelchair beside me—

+

Dear Lord in your back room,
in your white jacket and gloves:

                the room spins
when you stick the electric pin in,

                  when you turn on the charge
so it sparks at the tip.

            The hands flex and grip—

the monkey can't help it—

Is this what the awe is about?
Night and stars in a monkey's skull?

Those instruments spread out on a cart,
                                        their ambivalent
glittering?
          (The sound of that cart being wheeled down the hall.)

+

Mountains spreading under a dome of sky—

+

In the end, there was only pain for him.
The bones in his back decayed
                              so he winced.
He couldn't get up to pee, so I held his cock in my hand,
aimed it into a bowl I found by his bed.

I patted his claw.
              My father had receded far from me,

the starburst and glitter in his skull

          grown windy and dim.

He looked too small
beneath the bed's wrinkled landscape,
a useless, nearly

      emptied animal.

The World You Inhabit

Because they couldn't leave him in the road,
the boys propped the old man in the driver's seat
and pushed his car off the bridge.
The headlights glowed milkily in the black lake,
then, when they reached a certain depth, flickered out.
The radio, too, stopped singing that happy song.
All the way down to the lake's bottom, the car
couldn't believe the strange thing that was happening to it,
how the old man would not roll up the window,
would not turn the key, how water filled it completely.
That night, while those boys spent his money on women in Tulsa,
his car rocked deep into silt and mud.
The old man's arms floated emptily at his sides
unsure of what to do with themselves,
while high above him, in the world you continue to inhabit,
raindrops decorated the lake's surface.

Giving It Back

An abandoned child by the gas pumps who said nothing,
a child who stared down the highway into the sun.

My life, which I have to give back.

Didn't see who left her, the station owner told the very young cop

while they walked her into the convenience store
and she ran her fingers over the brilliant candy rows.

My life, which I'm supposed to give back.

The cop unfolded his cell phone and
What kind of people would just drive off like that? the station owner said.

Such a pretty child, such a breath—
and my life, which I will have to give back,

which I'm supposed to return to You—

+

Everybody gives it back, Augustus blue-lipped in bed,
an unusual chill that summer, endless light rain,

or the hard winter of Aachen and Charlemagne at his window
admiring the snow, he'd felt so good that morning,

but now the fever returned.

Julian speared by his troops in the blinding sun.
Strychnine-veined, sweat-addled in his tent, Alexander among Chaldeans—

I could have given mine back under the fluorescent lights
where I came to buy cigarettes,

where that little blond-haired girl
has been growing wings this entire poem—

+

My father gave it back in Cleveland while snow
buried every car beneath the hospital window.

I watched the nurses grow winged,
watched them hover whitely above his body.

We must return what we have taken,
we must give back what we received,

and when he exhaled at last—
like an animal, low and guttural—

the nurses fluttered at the window,
they took his breath into the snow.

+

Thus, even my father returned what had been lent him—

and that little girl grows more beautiful
as she recedes into memory—

how they set her on the counter,
and she never said a word.

How I stood beside the magazine rack, five dollars in my hand,
and watched her flex those blinding wings,

how an hour later they would find the note in her pocket,

and would learn the way her father gave his life back
two miles up the road by the lumberyard,

site of personal despair, site of his return.

That little girl rose quietly into the air,
and her wings obscured the ceiling, they canceled out the lights.

I must give it back, I must return it to You,
I cannot hold onto this life forever.

Four Theological Conversations

What's in that pot? Lamb stew with carrots and potatoes. *What's in that other pot?* That other pot is empty. *And this one here? And that one there?* Empty, empty. *And what's in the refrigerator?* Perishables. *Perishables?* Things that wilt and die. *And what's in the drawer?* The knives I use to slice the perishables.

Is it bleeding? It's just a little cut. *Is it bleeding bad?* No, not really. I just nicked myself with this knife. *You should hold it under cold water. You should cover it in gauze or paper towel. Do you have any alcohol? Do you have any Neosporin cream? You should wrap it in cloth. You should tie it off at the joint so the bleeding stops.*

Thank you Lord for this food we're about to eat. *Has the bleeding stopped?* And thank you Lord for our friends who love us. *I can see a spot there, on the gauze.* And thank you, also, for the many kindnesses of the day. *It's like a perishable unfolding its petals. It's like a lamb's red eye opening. It'll scare the children.*

It was a good stew. Thank you. *Is there more?* No. *And how is your cut?* The bleeding's stopped. *And the knife?* Safe in its drawer. *And the perishables?* Asleep in the crispers. *And the perishables?* All tucked away in the crispers. *And the per-ishables?* They are dreaming and happy. *And the children?* As I said, they're asleep.

Transcendentalism

The headless man is balancing
a red balloon on his shoulders
as if I wouldn't notice.

Now he is raking leaves in his yard.
Now he rests on the porch steps,
pretending to eat a sandwich.

I think I could get used to the headless man
and those pretty eyes he's markered on.

I think I could come to love that balloon
bobbing knowingly in the cool breezes
that drift from the distant, mist-soaked mountains.

There is sunset, then sunset, then sunset,
each one richer than the last,
and I think about sitting on his porch steps,

my head nestled in that warm space
between his shoulder and the balloon.

The headless man is afraid of needles, hairpins, pencils, cats.
He smiles beautifully,
then rises from the steps and picks up his rake.

Look at the slip of ribbon
that fastens the balloon to his neck.
Should I cut it? Would that be transcendence?

The Believer

Only his old dog recognized him when,
after twenty years,

Odysseus returned to Ithaka.
Sometimes I am nothing

but a bit of dirt ground into the floor.
Oh, darling, darling,

the waitresses don't say to me,
wiping down the tables after a long day.

So, one by one, Odysseus dispatched the suitors
as some girl might scrub me away

with soap and an old rag,
violently. I want to be violently

rubbed out. Rub me out,
God. Once, Odysseus' dog had been,

in Lattimore's translation,
very clever at tracking, but now

he was in bad times, ragged and dying. Still,
he tapped his tail to greet his long absent

master. The scrub brush enters the beer glass
the way I want God to enter

me—to clean me out.
The girls sweep the floor, then straighten the chairs.

Odysseus' dog ate scraps the suitors discarded
and as that dog died,

Odysseus smiled down at him fondly.
God's attention also comes as light

from above. It's time to go now, time to go.
Dark outside. He was, Homer says, a loyal dog,

but what am I supposed to eat?
This book of stories?

The Adulterer

Thinking to have their fun, those boys
set a match to the kerosene-soaked
rabbit
      then watched it blaze across the lawn
and into the garage
            where it thumped
and smoldered behind the wheelbarrow—

+

and so it also entered the memory
of the girl who watched
from her bedroom window

but never spoke of it to anyone—

+

and, *They were going to skin it and eat it, anyway,*
I told myself, having stopped at my desk
to think about the scene
I'd just invented.

Don't mind me, said the little voice
at the back of the garage.

Then, silence. Tools and a ladder.

I've done terrible things,
I said into the black garage.

+

The rabbit's scream stayed in the boys' ears
long after the scuttling in the garage
had ceased.
            One of them laughed
uneasily. Then another. *Who's going
to go in there and fetch that cooked rabbit?*
the first asked.

+

Her parents kept many rabbits in cages on the porch.
The girl had learned not to give them names.

Sometimes she even went with her mother
to sell their meat at the market—

so why was she crying?

+

I forgive you,
said the little voice from behind the wheelbarrow.

It's not right, said the girl in her room,
looking out the window at the boys
who stood beneath the porch light

                         laughing.

You, whom I have wronged, are in the kitchen
making me dinner. A clatter of pans,

and now you're singing, your voice
drifting up the stairs, I can hear it where I sit
at my desk

+

in the black garage.
                    That's how love
works, I said to the wheelbarrow and tools,
being, at that moment, in love

                              with someone,

not you.

+

And after another moment, the smallest boy
was made to carry the charred and smoking
meat
        out into the open on a shovel.
They buried it in the garden where no one
would ever find it—

+

For many years, the girl and her mother
brought meat faithfully to the market.

And when she was older, she snapped
and skinned the rabbits herself.

There's no explaining a marriage, I said,

+

hunched behind the wheelbarrows
among cobwebs.

Stop rationalizing,
said the voice from its hole.

You had finished cooking our dinner.
Hello, you called from the bottom of the stairs. *Hello?*

By now, the girl had turned off the bedroom light
and the boys had crossed her black lawn

                                  into memory.

It burned for a while, and then I felt
nothing at all.

Trying to Forget About You

In the distant future,
every place is either hallway or room.

In the distant future,
you have been dead for a thousand years.

I wear my people's white uniform
and tell the hover car my destination.

The shock of artificial sunlight
through virtual windows
                              is lovely—
how it tingles my skin.

In the distant future,
                      they upload news to my brain
so I know what to say about my enemy.

We built such enormous guns on the moon.

On the public screens,
                        I watch the glittering missiles
rise airlessly from the lunar surface.

Room or hallway, room or hallway

is all we have in the distant future, our constructions
crusting over the planet—

and I slip through them
like a clot through a man
who doesn't know his time has come.

In the future,
            you are never in my thoughts,
and I love my disastrous country
                        instead.

Darling, in the future,
            you are impossible to remember
sitting on your sofa with your cat
reading a book.
            The way you fasten your white robe
with a mismatched sash,
then pour yourself another drink
while the cat licks its paws
            is unknown to me.

Some days, I take the elevator to the highest room
where the actual sun

                    streams through skylights.

No one goes there anymore,
the screen long defunct, the furniture of a dead age.

(My people retreated lower and lower,
digging new rooms into the earth.)

I live in the future the way
memories live in your mind—

and you inhabit my mind the way
utopia lives in the machinery of governance.

I wish you could see the enemy's primitive bombs
explode above our force fields

                    like the orange chrysanthemums
I watched you worry over
one specific Sunday morning

              ages ago.

[   ]

Cookie, I can hear them scratching in those walls.
All night long they say *scritch, scritch, scritch*.
Hush now. Hush. [   ]
                                        There you go.
They're OK, they don't mean no harm, anyways.
Not to you nor me.
                        Coming out of the wall sockets
quick as sparks. Got those little claws on them.

+

Some days it snows all night. Then they sleep
like the deadened. Like your dear old dad.
Tell the truth. You can hear them. I knowed it.
Scritch scritch like a rocking chair.
                                And rain
on the roof will wake them up. And thunder
sets them going good.

+

I do miss him. That's true. [

] Yes, I do. [

]

+

You don't need to tell me nothing. You don't
need to visit.
        When night comes down I got
all the company I need.
               [   ] Boy,
a little silence is good for the soul. Sometimes,
they're so feisty I sleep in the yard. No need
to bring me in no more. [   ]
                  Hear that now?

Menhirs

I was lying on the couch
and outside rain kept falling
so I turned the page of my magazine
while Mary hummed in the bedroom,
changing the sheets.
On television, a man went on about
dead empires. What was he saying?
Piles of stones, long stone walls
winding through the green fields of,
I guessed England, then
several mysterious stone circles
in the center of which were—
I knew what they were called—
menhirs. The television was
muted and the man moved his lips
again, perfectly comfortable
among the stones and wind,
in his tweed jacket, his bright red tie.
Mary was still humming,
pushing the beds back into place.
Once again, the sheets were
clean and smelled of soap.
Outside, the rain came down
in vast populations and now

I was slipping into sleep,
raindrops exploding on the windows,
wind leaning into the walls. That week,
a young woman I knew slightly
had drowned. They'd towed her empty boat
through the storm. I must write her family,
I thought from far away. Then, a sense,
like a warm wind, settled against me:
we drift through time
the way trees drift through rain.
We hold none of it. We hold
none of it. I felt terrified
in the bright room. On TV,
the man was still talking.
Mary pointed the remote control at him
to change the channel.
For a moment longer
menhirs glowed in the sunset.

The Search

Soon it will be time to give up the search

(flashlights knifing through tangled branches,
a reporter on the roadside brushing snow from his eyes,
saying to the camera,

The old lady slipped past the nurses again,

saying,

She won't stop searching for her dead husband—)

Mothy snow has filled her footprints.
A kind of love story, a kind of

nightgown

drifting through brambles—
snow that sifts from her braincase
through black trees—

he must have gone off without his coat again,
he will catch cold

out here in the weather—

Over the ridge, TV trucks glow.
Our flashlights turn falling snow

into insects—

91

Then, one of us holds up a wet pink heart.
Over here, he calls, *over here*,
and through the woods, the beams converge,

but it is only her soiled slipper.
We should go home.
                    I will never know love,

or have such love.
My skin will grow slack over knobby bones
until I'm translucent.

The woods brighten and become infinite,
that old woman running through them,

—white inner space—
she who couldn't stop her husband
from walking
                    right into a blizzard.

An Old Man

It was a sad car
the sun couldn't soothe
the shattered windshield
someone had shot holes
in the driver's side door
it had no wheels
propped up on blocks
behind the barn
where the old dog
slept in the glare
rusted hulk
that could not speak
without a radio
just wires in its mouth
key long ago discarded
in a tattered coat's
unchecked pocket
look how the edifying rain
has done a number on you
only the farm children
dreaming of race cars
will play in your wrecked
interior.

The Future

More than anything
               the old man loved his only son
so on weekends, against his young wife's wishes,
he flew that strange boy
                  high above the city
in his Cessna Skyhawk.
                 Up through the snow squalls
into turbulent clouds
                so the boy laughed when the plane
shook
     and, *Look*, the old man said, *look*, where the clouds
parted
     and there were the tall towers, there
was the highway thick with cars,
                 there
was the neighborhood of his youth
                  grown new and sprawling,
swimming pools and shopping centers.
It was such a pleasure
             to show his son these things
that when his heart stopped, who could deny
that the old man,
            high above the city of his childhood,
died happy?

+

    Hello? the boy said into the radio.
Hello? pressing the green button, then the black one,
the airplane having retained

                its equilibrium.
But he could not work the radio,

                      could not answer
the worried voices,

            the plane skimming above the rooftops
and highways.

          Hello? he said, punching the buttons again,
speaking into the fist-size

              microphone.

+

Hello, the treetops answered

                as the plane roared past.
Hello, the rooftops called,

             shuddering in the wind
and snow.

      And the nation, which listened to the news,
rushed to its thousand windows to watch him pass.

95

And *Isn't it strange*, the nation decided,
how we are, all of us, hurtling onward? And

                        Isn't it lovely

how the past recedes into white distances,

                    lovely boy

with his face pressed to the glass

                  while the city thinned—

+

Harmless

        darling boy, we thought—his plane like a toy.
We caught him on our camera phones,
compiled him to the Web.

                And how will it end?

the Internet asked, voice of billions.
Into a building or down in a field?

                Pixilated child,

his father, like any of us, sunk deep into his happy past,
cheek to the window

            where he slept his last. And the scene-
comprehending hard drives purred and clicked
as the airplane crossed our screens—

+

         and lit our rooms
with blue.
    I was one of those who waved
from my front porch as he roared past. *Hello,*
I called, *hello,*
       and thought I caught a sadness in his face
that later I observed more slowly on my screen.

Many times, I watched him
slide past snow squalls and the harbor
until, far from shore, his engine dead at last,
the speck of him slipped downward
        into the glassy ocean.

Acknowledgments

Thanks to the editors of the following publications, where most of these poems have appeared: Academy of American Poets, *AGNI, Boulevard, Copper Nickel, Ecotone, Explosion-Proof, Field: Contemporary Poetry & Poetics, The Journal, The Kenyon Review, The Literary Review, The Missouri Review, The New England Review, NOR: the New Ohio Review, The Paris Review, Plume, The Plume Poetry Anthology, Poetry, Poetry Daily, A Public Space, The 2016 Pushcart Prize Anthology, The Southern Review, & The Virginia Quarterly Review;*

and to early critics of these poems, Hadara Bar-Nadav, Noah Blaustein, Sharon Bryan, Teresa Cader, Martha Collins, Mary Y. Hallab, Tony Hoagland, Joy Katz, Dana Levin, Wayne Miller, Alan Michael Parker, and Jonathan Weinert.

This book is for Michael and Lynn, good friends.

Publication of this book was made possible by grants and donations. We are also grateful to those individuals who participated in our 2017 Build a Book Program. They are:

Anonymous (6), Evan Archer, Sally Ball, Jan Bender-Zanoni, Zeke Berman, Kristina Bicher, Laurel Blossom, Carol Blum, Betsy Bonner, Mary Brancaccio, Lee Briccetti, Deirdre Brill, Anthony Cappo, Carla & Steven Carlson, Caroline Carlson, Stephanie Chang, Tina Chang, Liza Charlesworth, Maxwell Dana, Machi Davis, Marjorie Deninger, Lukas Fauset, Monica Ferrell, Emily Flitter, Jennifer Franklin, Chuck Gillett, Dorothy Goldman, Dr. Lauri Grossman, Naomi Guttman & Jonathan Mead, Steven Haas, Mary Heilner, Hermann Hesse, Deming Holleran, Nathaniel Hutner, Janet Jackson, Christopher Kempf, David Lee, Jen Levitt, Howard Levy, Owen Lewis, Paul Lisicky, Sara London & Dean Albarelli, David Long, Katie Longofono, Cynthia Lowen, Ralph & Mary Ann Lowen, Donna Masini, Louise Mathias, Catherine McArthur, Nathan McClain, Gregory McDonald, Britt Melewski, Kamilah Moon, Carolyn Murdoch, Rebecca & Daniel Okrent, Tracey Orick, Zachary Pace, Gregory Pardlo, Allyson Paty, Marcia & Chris Pelletiere, Taylor Pitts, Eileen Pollack, Barbara Preminger, Kevin Prufer, Vinode Ramgopal, Martha Rhodes, Roni & Richard Schotter, Peter & Jill Schireson, Soraya Shalforoosh, Peggy Shinner, James Snyder & Krista Fragos, Megan Staffel, Alice St. Claire-Long, Robin Taylor, Marjorie & Lew Tesser, Boris Thomas, Judith Thurman, Susan Walton, Martha Webster & Robert Fuentes, Calvin Wei, Abby Wender, Bill Wenthe, Allison Benis White, Elizabeth Whittlesey, Hao Wu, Monica Youn, and Leah Zander.